a guide to tongue tie surgery

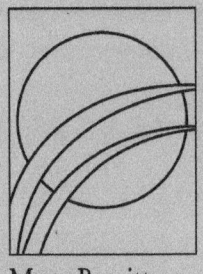

Mary Burritt Christiansen Poetry Series

Mary Burritt Christiansen Poetry Series
Hilda Raz, Series Editor

The Mary Burritt Christiansen Poetry Series publishes two to four books a year that engage and give voice to the realities of living, working, and experiencing the West and the Border as places and as metaphors. The purpose of the series is to expand access to, and the audience for, quality poetry, both single volumes and anthologies, that can be used for general reading as well as in classrooms.

For additional titles in the Mary Burritt Christiansen Poetry Series, please visit unmpress.com.

a guide to tongue tie surgery

UNIVERSITY OF
NEW MEXICO PRESS
ALBUQUERQUE

poems

Tina
Carlson

© 2023 by Tina Carlson
All rights reserved. Published 2023
Printed in the United States of America

ISBN 978-0-8263-6524-8 (paper)
ISBN 978-0-8263-6525-5 (e-book)

Library of Congress Cataloging-in-Publication data
is on file with the Library of Congress

Founded in 1889, the University of New
Mexico sits on the traditional homelands of the
Pueblo of Sandia. The original peoples of New
Mexico—Pueblo, Navajo, and Apache—since time
immemorial have deep connections to the land
and have made significant contributions to the
broader community statewide. We honor the land
itself and those who remain stewards of this land
throughout the generations and also acknowledge
our committed relationship to Indigenous peoples.
We gratefully recognize our history.

Cover art by Lene Kilde; photograph by Lisbeth
Lund Andresen
Designed by Isaac Morris
Composed in Minion, Medusa

For Tres

"Why, why," she cried, "can one of them
Speak words of love and the other has no tongue
To speak at all?"
— Ovid

The thing we are trying to say
Is in the language of leaves
— Linda Gregg

Our motto is gather
— Annemarie Ni Churreain

Contents

There I Stood, in All My Forms

Backyard of Her Alphabets

Ghost Town on Iris Avenue

Those were days when roads fired up
and brothers rammed their bikes
into the door. Everything too hot
to touch and the fancy man with a red car,

hair greased back slick, gave me a swim.
Trees were left to their own devices.
Each mountain pressed against

the other. Believe me when I say
the full moon loosened the dressings
on my mother's memory. All
her mouths started talking at once.

Comets flew through the shadow
of worm moon. Wars were waged
against wood and fists made parents.
There was a sky that never fell, but grew

white as bandages. I want to say
body as if it matters. The town fell
to its knees. Heaven turned to
smoke in those ghost churches.

A Guide to Tongue Tie Surgery

Say excavation, exoneration.
My mother's mouth, washed out

with soap. In that cool cocoon
a salmon caught in stones.

Bird flapping in a trap. Cheek
swab, sea snail. Show me

how a smile hides argument
behind its teeth. Ask her,

what words made your
crimes? She ate wood,

sampled leather. Grazed
the backyard of her alphabets.

Grass cats lumbered the clods
of her thoughts. We tumbled

through her silent gardens,
filled them with noise.

To untether the tongue,
say frenulum. Say frenzy.

A simple snip and drop
of blood. Let her taste

peaches, warm June. I imagine
my mother is more than apology,

flag planted in her throat
unfurled past mumble and scorn.

Poplar at dawn, she is lingual.

My Mother as Moon

Though I stormed the weathered

blood of her ancestors, I wanted milk
when I arrived. She promised food but

fed me iron. I starved. I dimmed into slack.

I wanted to be daughter and she said,
mother me. I was born in an asylum

of dawn, stream of light in my mouth.

I was transfixed by the pines
and all their green hands. On

ground blurred with dirt, quartz

gleamed like gristle. Now she nods out,
bent petals on stem, cratered leg crimson.

I tend the relics of her wounds.

Cigarette Smoke and a Blue Impala

My grandmother finds me dreaming again. *You work too much, darlin'*, she lilts, and the dream shifts to cigarette smoke and a blue Impala. She is driving me to the movies and I am a prisoner on parole. *You eating okay, darlin'? You in love?* She takes a long drag and we stop for some gin. I never know what my crimes are. *My work makes me sink*, I say. *Too many people wanting pills to calm down.* My grandmother grew up on a Texas horse ranch and her stepfather was named Fate. She spent her young adulthood in a sanatorium coughing up blood. Not much gets her down. *Think of it this way, darlin' of mine. You just have to love them and they will feel better.* I inhale her smoke and calm down. There are so many flowers blooming in the road. My life of crime sits in the back seat now. My grandmother, now transparent, throws me a kiss, and her Impala, blue as sky, drops me off in my bed.

Gran Via
Spain, 1973

I left home for a courtyard of kitchens,
the scent of cook smoke, olive oil.
Women sang at the stove, echoing
in open windows.
We smoked *tabaco negro*, Ducados.
On his blue scooter, Veli zipped
around ancient corners, wet
with wash water.
I thought I knew something
until Franco roughed the air
with his armies.

We were young,
García Lorca still missing.
Four hundred thousand killed in camps, cantos.
We were not allowed on the grass in parks;
barefoot, we waded in fountains.
There were lakes and leaky boats.
In the Prado, a man playing guitar
until I turned into rain. We lived
in trains, dark flats
with elevators grated in rust.

Chocolate thick as mud, churros.
Los Años de Hambre.
Vermouth, *mariscos*, tanks wide as the street.
Emilia, Mireya, Avelino, Antonio.
Guardia Civil on every corner
didn't blink in uniform.

That was the year Neruda died in Isla Negra.
Watergate.
Brown hills to the north, Nescafé.
Tortilla española, mercados.
Old women on a park bench wrapped in black
shawls. One called me daughter.
Galletas. On a hitchhike to Portugal,
a man without a windshield sped
to Lisboa. Rocky coastlines. The sun
scorched everything it touched.

Agoraphobia

My father was afraid to be born.
The womb, full of ghosts: hearty
Swedes digging snow caves in woolen
pants, and those Germans always
building new cities. Not to mention the sister
who dead-fish floated the year
before. In that roiling cave, my father
thrashed, roped to his mother's
pulse. Weeks late, he was born in a blizzard.
The air teamed with frozen flakes.
Her skin smelled of vinegar and sweat.

My Father Comes Home from War with Guns

blossoming in the muck of memories.
A ruin in ranks still cracking jokes

about his hands turned to smoke.
He paws the door of his mother's

home, its trenches veiled with lace, pickling
fruit like eyes, souring in their juices. How he

bruises her with want, her hands silent
in their flowered pockets. He sees meadows

in her arms, the dark bar of a shadow, shade.
He is no longer her half-daughter, for he has killed.

She cannot touch him, will not. Each stone
she has planted is a grave.

Blown open, he has never longed like this.
There is no cool breeze or song

to rally the gods. This is a moment
after generations of war. She will say

it was a reunion of graces, of prayer.
My father's heart cindered on that porch.

My Father Prayed

My father prayed to the gods of snow,
a white crown on his hand-hewn
home, how the brown heat
of that wood turned to glass,
turned sacred and silent in the dripping
dark. Unlike my mother, who loved
thick books sandwiched in pews,
hymns wafting through her thin ribs,
her brow wet with sweat for the divine.
A scientist died and said, *There is*
no god. Just particles, animated, and
the invisible. My father skied the mountains
of his years, still wearing the wools of war,
his face lit with the ice of his heaven.

Mud Babies

Before we were born, my father sculpted us of muck. Only indentations for eyes so we would never see the battles in his. Sludge of handprints on our mother's vast belly.

Later my brother cried so hard he turned blue. I was deciduous like the cottonwoods gleaming next door. I was the absence of luster, bark covered. I loved the mud that was my mother. My hungry beginnings on the ground in fall, childhood's season rife with punch and gun.

Once the sky opened her eyes and saw me. A small tree, rooting in the dirt. I was lumber in a breeze. My father cut me down under stars so bright his hands lit up. I was cavern, cabin to his dreams. He lived in me for the rest of his days.

The Embassy of Silence

My mother fills paper
boats with pastel mints,
juice glasses with bourbon.
The room shimmers with lit
cigarettes. We watch
the perfumed players sneak
peeks, bet and bluff. Out back
my father beats hedges
with rusted shears, says,
God damn shit ass.
Glasses empty. My brother
puts frozen peas on his bruises.
My mother hums in her new
blue party dress. Ladies praise
her close-to-perfect white cake.

At the Rest Stop, Fully Gloved, She Calls Me Mommy

Mercy descends from grey drapes
of rain on the horizon. She enters

the shrine "For Disabled Only,"
doesn't come out for ages. Wind
turns my hat into a bird. I taste
metal and salt in the air. Here's to

the Goddess of Soap and Water,
to gloves and the imaginary safety

we don. I call out, *Please keep your
gloves on and unlock the door,*

and a man gives me a look. She
emerges, relieved and smiling. She is

blooming into the season of death, just as
some have rehung Christmas stars to scare off

the plague. She hands me her wrist,
and I pull one glove off cleanly. Then

with that just-bared hand, she
fingers the other, still gloved,

all the threat and germ of it, touches it
like she did each couch and corner of her

left home, her cinnamon jar, her old blue
chair. Rest-stop trucks groan and puff in unison.

There is no grace to this attempt
at duty. I mother her the best I can.

She elevates her swollen feet
in the back seat of the car.

You Will Dream That Great Aunt Dolor
Loves Your Wild Hair

Your son will greet you at the gate.
Slicked with sleep, he knows
nothing of sandspits or cannulas.
Forget your smoky bars
as these green days play for
free. Pileated, you will beam
and feed. Ditches thread
the meandering rivers. You will
dream that great aunt Dolor
loves your wild hair, sends
songs from the old country. We
promise a return to the time
before fist-shattered glass on your
father's grave. No lack of mothering
air, no gin-bottle mornings,
no kickball head injuries.
You have not been cursed, nor has
the boy you will come to know.

Dark Dowry

How holy the cloth sewn sidewise

from doll clothes, paw prints,
shreds of dresses threaded tight,
the flowered curtain
of her sick bed, pond stink,
continents of jungle grass,
flakes of lava and snow, fingernails,
ice plant, sea shell and corn stalk.
Even the sheen of the mica
mine, a snakeskin, meteors, cake
recipes: her quilt woven and wearing
thin. And what of her core's endurances,
crystalline, tumorous, glossy
fat clogging its blood?
The planets were formed
by collision, then the back
of her mother riding away
with Fate. It is thought
the earth is mostly vapors
of stone, so hot they
can make a moon with
divided light, skin so
thick, uninhabitable.

Sheltering in Place for Beginners

Are you awake? You have relied on anesthesia during
the scalpel's trusty removals. In the ice melt of morning

sit still, read jokes. Wind predicts drought. You will grow
strong in your heart's ribbed hospital. Become

the blue rising up over your bed. Wake to smell a skunk,
touch the skin of breath. Enjoy the crows' caw

from their branches. Under the spruce, taste something salty.
Let loneliness grow feathers. In your brain, an amygdala

howls through cracked glass. There she hunkers, memorizing
danger. Embody the lost lover's voice, temporary

as an amber sun before the heavy machinery of night.
In enviable dark, shake the hand of sleep and let go.

Coat-Grave, Nation of Moths

Born hinged and hewn
library of scent and
spent bark.

As daughter

Coat-grave, nation of moths
lashed fast to the wick

of her wood, crusts
of photos and thread.

I learned early

Dark dowry, cloaked
as a nun.

to fold the pink

Cat-ash, baby

heat of my tongue

teeth. Open like a spell,

place it there, among

the shroud of wings

whiff her wood.
It still smells young.

neat and dumb
as a glove

Motes of ghosts
thin in the air.

ALMA
(atacama large millimeter/submillimeter array)

We were girls in the scent
paths of ants, wet shoes,
cigarette-lit. Knew dirt
was alive, life all pulp
and bone, blind as buds
on the branches.

Now your azimuth is always
up. All eyes on the sky.
Desert bound, wide faced,
hold the new bodies of suns
as they flower into fire.

I miss telling you about love,
how to fall in the dark.
We sat in the rash of light
between window and gate.

In your granular view,
do the heavens still breathe?

In this dry time we say
Atacama. We say sky
flicked with light, say
temporary.

We wanted the sky to speak
of what is not to be
contained. Now, parabolic,
what do you thirst for?

Did you know that starving girls
were found naked in a tub?

That whole families are fleeing
into the sea?

You, on your rollers and spacers,
tended to by tiny men, your black
holds, fissures, pulsar sweeps.

Through the fawn-soft light of universes
planets herd dust and ice into blue
rings. O ALMA, there was a time
we were alive, promised quick
lanes to heaven. Gracious,
our salvation.

Anatomy of Silence

Confess: The firstborn bears the weight of words caught in her parents' dark throats. There is a flaw in the fireplace of their bed, and their dreams sift the still air for sin, song, salt. When she is born, they feed her blood. She learns the hymnal of hematocrit. *Take this, then we will never speak of it again.*

Panpipe: Inhale the dark long hallways with closed doors, the cloister of the body's caverns. The opposite of a red hymnal behind the pew. Exhale the music bones make deep in their marrow when dancing.

Pronoun: What we pass around on a plate and offer to strangers. The certainty of coins in a wishing well. I am she and she is they. He says touch, she says grab. In Spanish *dawn* is female, as in that light that begins us.

Battle: Revenge starts fires in our mind. Burns up the stories containing a hope of water. Once she was bled, the ancestors had a heyday building a ship for drowning. Even the sky has eyes.

Alien: You are what you eat, the teacher tells small children. Once she exits the schoolyard, she chews on fallen leaves. Like wings they float through her. She lives in a tribe of pollinators. Listen to the languages that haunt her. Siphon the code words for ghost and bone, rupture, escape.

Fin Feather Bark and Skin

Truth be told, we live in the depths of an ocean of air.
Bottom suck the muck of our lives, rely on those with
bark to breathe. Palolo worms are luminous at the surface
of waters. Wind roots for the girl who is storm whirled
above the earth on the back of her horse, drops back down
still snug in the saddle. Herds of cows fly like geese in a
mackerel sky. Listen to the trees breeze in fall and you,
too, will rise up.

Come out, O you attic trunks and firetips. You saddle girls
and fog fish, potted plants, you sea worms melting in light.
We are drowning in our air ocean. Simmered to a boil,
punching holes in our sky, waging war with our kin.
What sleeve of snow can save us now?

Day after America

1.

Unearthed rot. The ride a sheathed childhood. Unsheathed, he slicks
his thumb along the narrow tracks of my mouth while winter is diesel
fumed. A train hurtles where we have never met. Have only met his
scent: sour, of snow. Soured, I spend my time sick up the slope. Trees
silent.

2.

Ruin. I sit groaning at 5:00 a.m. I am a dress of my own skin. Mother
enters my dream through automatic doors, waves good-bye to birds
in my head. Under the mask, I am still piano, fingering bone keys.
Bony, I am made of flowers under your feet. Fence after wind. I want
shade under fractured branches, the birds breathing, birds breathing.
Soon, we will all be America. Underfoot: teeth, tiny blue truck, stoic
as stone. Breathing in holy nests I hang onto the. Hang on the.

Metronome and Daruma Doll

Dear Daruma Doll,
I yearn for sight, for eyes. Rhythms
rile me, I am encased.

There once was a girl
who tried to match my beat; I
ran from her fingers, wild.

Dear metronome,
I once could roll, regain
my stature. For centuries
I have hoped and burned.

I waited for painted eyes,
first a wink then
full stare.

Ichi—the pulse in your neck
Ni—a prayer you once sang to the girl
San—the movements of her fingers across the keys

Dear Daruma,
I am unwound yet alive. My dream:
to be unarmored, speed up
and slow down,

to be tide, clock, blood pulse in
the wrist of a child.

Four—tempo of cranes in flight
Five—fingers on my case, so light
Six—dust motes made by the sun, marking time

Dear metronome,
You are a marching band, grandfather
of clocks. My father stared at the wall
for centuries without a blink. Once he

cut his eyelids off so he wouldn't fall
asleep. Sometimes we aim too high
and lose sight of the goal. Your

music is sap, is wood root wrung
from water underground.

My Daruma, my doll,
I am dreaming your face.
Once I ticked through
Beethoven, then to a

tap. Once spiders lay
eggs in my struts. I see
your father staring at the
wall, a shy god

captured in paint. I know
my mother was oak,
was forested deep in
cold until I was born,
cut deep from her trunk.

Dearest 'Nome,
What do we know? Devotion of
monk and tree, we are functional.
The hands that paint and play us

have forgotten our names. You
choose the tempo, I'll lead
the dance. I may fall, but I'm up
more times than I'm down.

Sichi—There is grief in my eyes
Hachi—a Kata and well-placed punch
Ku—Taste of salt, of sweat, the sea

Dearest doll,
My joints are old and stiff.
Some years I sit silent and
face the wall, waiting for the

gods to speak. Paint eyes
on my face, so I
can see yours.

Ten—still as a stance

As the Numbers of Dead Rise, Moths Fill the Room

Dead leaves still staunch
on stalks are like moths, breathing

the green light of spring: moths
that silken the lamp, flap the bulb,

harmonize in the night's
wind garden with hum

and drumbeat of wings.
I was once a moth

folded in some book yellowed
and torn, so close to mouth

in the wet bed of imagination.
The woman who died

holding her child's hand is now
moth, like all the dead, turning

the page of this day with
their numbers, rooting

for juice, for the lost shelter of skin
and cracks of light through the sill.

Lampshade and Floor Mat

Dear floor mat,
When the warden sank,
gods sang the psalm of his
drowning, the bewilderment of
skin in descent.

Dear lampshade,
Have you ever seen the blue
sleeve of the sky? You are
soft moon in the room's dark
nights. Bulb of skull.
Little drum of light.

Dear mat,
I was taken to the
dank cave of the man who
gave orders, held sway.
I was made to shade his
glare. Who has not heard
the hum of him, felt the
sweaty palms
and grim sin of yank
and pull away?

Dear shade,
I know the feet of the missing
and craved. Everyone wants
to be welcomed. I too am guilty:

have harbored mud when
I should have confessed. I suffer
from a theft of breath. The sand

those gods have given me
is salt. How they trudge and
sink in the mire of me.

Dear floor mat,
You are footprint and maw. Small sea-
bed at the door, salted and tattered.
When you are put in the bin and taken
to waste, will you simmer in the sun?
Become silt?
Shoes line up in your honor.

Dear lampshade,
I have left
//////\\\\
myself at the door

I apologize for my crimes
I confess
(((())))

Dear mat,
I was charged with not being useful
enough. Cells opened, and I was set
free: a candle's cloak.

Here are the small coins of light
left inside. My last
offerings: to the feet and paws

you mold, your matted
lack, the magnificent
mud you keep.

Turn the Ship Around

Saint Ursula

Turn the ship around
for the holiness
of open water:

your beam and mast,
magnificent. Take girls keening
on the street into your deep
cloak of a sail and set out where

storms of the sea seethe. You believe
in the gods of wind and waves.

The cloistered girls. The men with
raised swords. Slaughter
is a shore where
armies wait, skulls line
the beaches, small lamps
of bone.

What potion brought
you here?

Be prayer, not prey,
in the sea's convent,
your craft's wood culled
from royal forests.

Cool the girls'
fevers with brine,
the heart's hull
star filled.

What is divinity if not
the horizon where
sun starves into dark?

Seabirds will choir you.

Anoint yourselves with
grit and salt, become
water, uncaptured.
Sainted, you will still
museums. Your

cloak so full of girls, your
bones that smell of almonds.

Heaven

1.

The first sorrow is a kind of silence under the sink. Such a dank place
to hide, dead spiders like husks of fallen stars.

This is where we meet. She, always making fun of my Spanish. Mountains
all around, sharper than teeth. We swim in the oceans of our mouths.

2.

In the shelter, a girl named Heaven mounts a revolt. She hates the
daily prayers, the jowls of the man with nails like claws. She hates that
godliness is a minister who pants in her ear,

thin pads on the floor, the women always
crying. Her spine all twisted and tied up.

Heaven says, *Dirt is only dirt. I have four rooms in my heart bigger
than a playground.*
Take the children out of the man's mouth, out of the cage's endless clanging.

Generations of silence inside us: births gone backward into spent eggs.
Her arms lined with cuts and scars. Flags for the missing and lost.

3.

So many sorrows to follow.

Sanctuary: foot rub, hawk call, reservoir of clean water.

Say the body
is a door,
and skin
makes immigration impossible.

We were once specks of light, *cielo.*
Horses painted on cool stone in the dark.

Snow Queen

1.

What should stay buried in times like these?
My skin is creased in the new mirror.
I have been kissed to death by too many.
Great and good, small and ugly, wicked and bad.

Snow melts. Steady drip, drip, drip
all day through the heat and light.

2.

Watch how I smooth the boy's hair,
tender him with tales as if they might
undress his innocence.

My mother did the same.
Dug for something hidden
under the new skin of her young.
An empty chair sits by the window.

Through the little hole, I see him watching.
Snowflakes grow larger and larger.
The moon is lit white gauze.
Soon we will guess at shapes under snow:
the rounded mound of a ball, a garden tool left out.

3.

My father went north looking for someone.
Strangers spoke in soft voices, invited him in.
He ate *kroppkakor* on tablecloths
painted with red flowers.
More cold than he ever dreamed.

When he was a boy,
his mother named him
after the girl who died at birth before him.
He tried to reach the high notes just for her.

The thicker the snow, the sharper the squint.
Something struck my eye, I cannot see you.
Glass fell out of the sky of his mother's eyes,
cloudy full moons. He led her around
on his arm. She sparkled
while her son-daughter
sang the way forward.
Linked together, glittering ice.

The past with its dank nest.
My father saved us gifts from the war.
His skin, with its snow and grit,
sleeping bags full of must.
A small grain of glass in his heart,
a gun.

The Little Robber Girl

Our home has cracked me into seasons: summer for stumps and stones, fall for the crow's caw, spring for glint on my blade, winter for what can turn on you.

All the men have gone. My names are *naughty wild ugly thing.* Mother drinks all day between her snoring naps. When she roasts a rabbit on the spit, bulldogs wrestle me for the bones.

I am the girl with dark eyes. When the golden girl arrives, I lust for her embroidered dress, her skin. She sleeps in my bed, and I watch the pulse dance in her neck.

Two loaves and a ham, sings my drunken ma. I wander a smoky hall, hungering. Mother stumbles about, and I pull at her beard.

The girl is looking for a boy she lost and loves. Birds fall from the limbs of my dreams, their feathers soft, though stiff.

I take her for a ride in her stolen coach, lit like a torch. How her eyes shine, dazzled at the fiery sky, my skill at the reins.

I will show her my wood pigeons, cooing in their cages, and my Reindeer Ba, who I tickle with my knife, bright-copper ring around his neck.

Look how I hold the bird to her lips and tell her to kiss. She does not know if she will live or die.

I let the girl go. Ba carries her across marshes and plains. She will find the boy and thaw his heart.

They will eat their golden soup, spin straw into gold, birth golden children who shine like the sun. I will grow cold as a blue crease of snow.

Monster

The judge is calm and caped, this room a dark shine, white walled, its pews smattered and smug. My lawyers seek to humanize me. They insist I do my hair like a child, ponytail bound, not blown like grass as he would have me. After the footage of my bound boys, the plunge, the lake-filled car: my head in my hands pretending to cry. I fed them well, have film to prove their smiling. If there was a crime, it was the gun of my past to my head, saying, *Do what I say, or I will kill you.* My stepfather's Christian hands on me, his smirk, his spit. My boys will never sit like this, legs crossed, charged. What lies between mother and monster? They peer then stare to see if I am sorry. I whisper to them in my dreams, that I am and I am not. I saved the boys from do-gooders going bad in the dark. I gave them truth: a good meal, return to water. I say I loved the smell of their heads in sleep. In my cell, their always-happy faces. Monster me if you will. But who among you has not drowned what you loved and turned from that shore convicted?

Open Your Mouth

with speculum dilator cannula the sterilized
doctor is huge and loud his wife subdued she suggests

we build snow caves don crampons climb glaciered volcanos
over ice cracking itself up into crevasses blue as bruise that

mouth words to chairs and scare the other customers

driving through a blizzard to see her too late teacups
laid out on cold tables chairs lined up for sale in

solitary they shaved her head gave her a dirty mat to sleep on
open your mouth pornographers hands always ungloved before

she sent a ring and a letter announcing her death I fall down start to
bleed
the ring must be buried under stone in a storm to stop the blood
what does it mean

to live on water after the dry fields of childhood books bloated with
mold
salt on skin rats on the pier souls afloat on the sound of the

long arm of the radiation machine breasts tattooed in blue

babies brought from the Hunan mountains on a late bus
carried by teen nannies impatient we smell strange

snow everywhere deep and soundless steep tea while
my daughter and I fly through the dark matter of space

in our magic craft see lights and strange shapes
I am afraid she is not we land on earth approach gates

my mother waits on the other side opens a tunnel to bypass the guards

Why did you kill your wife, mr XYZ?

She was a body, a voice, kept repeating herself. In the mirror the boy
was a form, a face, a hope. She was cold, an arm, repeating the mirror.
When I looked at the boy, his face, his hope, his ivory, she was saying,
Here, here.

How long had you planned the murder?

Since the trees started whispering, since the deer in the nets started
kicking, since I called and she came and I saw and she yielded to me.
Her winning words, her argument. Her echoes make fire in my head,
and I repeat, the deer were kicking, the nymphs laughing, and she
was arming her way through the trees, and the pond was a still face
who loved me and my fingers waiting.

Did you ever love her?

I remember the time I saw my ivory, my neck straining to kiss my
lips. Praising was praised, desiring was desired. My eyes my own
undoing. She was a stone, a voice, and I was a beautiful boy. He was
everything, yielding. I smiled and he smiled, I wept and he wept. The
nymphs, they fled. The deer were calling in the thickening trees, and
she was saying, *Here, here,* and I was in love with my own breath, his
retreat made me mad, my lips.

Do you feel remorse?

I beat my chest bloody for the warm water of his face. She was a stone,
a voice, but I was alive in him. Deer were dying and the trees falling
down, but his lips were my own and my face, his face, and my desire
only to yield and take at the same time. Soon, she was just a sound,
no body, no stone, and she kept saying, *Here, here,* and I look for him
under the frost I am burning.

Thirteen Children Rescued from Their Parents Testify

After I dream   in blood

I am cinched   bewildered

This new light

       a bowl
         of seeds

They call us

               saved

I cannot   remove the chain

Where

      the hungry convene   black

                birds flame

their wings   My sister's arms
          are thin she

holds small questions

        in her mouth

The smell of food
        in her fever

Burn me away from stairs covered

        in her

I cannot be pulled from the cliff's
                                        edge

                                                        of her breath

her bonnet
                                        made of scars

Ice Matron

You knit
blue sweaters
in the green heart of
Slovenia.

Red cars shone,
silver, salami, snow,
armored eyelashes.

You tied your girlish notes
to pieces of yarn and floated
them above the concrete. Your
father the mouthy mechanic,

your mother made dresses
of flour. Snow covered what
was done and not said with
tire irons and trains.

Floor plans for
the masses, or
fortune. You knit and knit
until you were
blue. Perfume ads
in purple lockers.

You never let him touch
the children. When you say
he is a good man,
your diamond
earrings flash their toothy
grins. Your spoons,
your alterations.

West Side Murders, Seven Years Later

1.

Tight-lipped police
Have the first bones
Call him Westside Bone Collector
Should look into a seedy stretch
Found rope and electrical tape on his

2.

He called me sugar, filled me with candy and smack. Called from his car across the windy street. I thought love was a vinyl seat in a clean car and a half hour under a tree. The branches filled with doves when he buried me in a dead volcano. Wind makes everything live again, even the frozen branches, even the town that will forget.

3.

Known to be violent
Still no sign
Absence of the park
Loved ones on their own
Daughter's bones were found

4.

When she was small, she cleaned the homes of her mother's men. Shocking, the sudden smell of bleach in her nose. Notice her hair, pulled back clean and black. She was called a good girl by the men who visited at night and tore her open. She wondered at the breath of sky, how huge and awake, even the extinct stars. How small she felt, her good-girl skin turned dangerous, called names she wasn't supposed to know. All of this before the weeds swallowed her, the dirt filled her eyes.

5.

He says, *But we are*, says, *Boys will be boys.* Things happen.

She says, *The heart is not a box of blood. It beats and beats through branches of the dead.*

6.

> Jamie Barela, age 15
> Monica Candelaria, age 22
> Victoria Chavez, age 26
> Virginia Cloven, age 24
> Syllania Edwards, age 15
> Cinnamon Elks, age 32
> Doreen Marquez, age 24
> Julie Nieto, age 24
> Veronica Romero, age 28
> Evelyn Salazar, age 27
> Michelle Valdez, age 22

7.

Spring comes, no matter what. Her green shoots slip through wet sleeves of ground, through branches bare as bone. Six women still missing: Darlene, Anna, Felipa, Nina, Shawntell, Leah. Birds nestle their names.

8.

Excavate

      Quarry

          Prey

             Pit

                Mine

                   Dig

Pulse

    Throb

        Pound

           Shudder

              Thump

                 Bleed

9.

Across the world, a whole village builds a grass raft to carry a sick woman and her new baby down the river to care.

Six woman are missing in our town. Eleven others and an unborn child call at night from the mouths of dead volcanoes.

Build me a raft, says the grass on their graves.

We sleep and dream, each extravagant breath extinct as a star on exhale.

How She Becomes a Fountain

Sorrow alternates with sunlight.

To kidnap a child,
start with her eyes,

irises round and
wide, and see

yourself there,
looking back

from the gaze cage
you have enjoyed

for centuries.
The child

will lose her
trail, will fold her

hands, will not turn
into a bird.

Find in her stashes
of gold the hymns

of whales, the
oceans turned

blue as plankton surrenders
to acid and heat. Light has no

destination.

You have left the ruins
steaming.

Let them keep the faces of girls
feathered and clawed.

She holds a bird,
her hands unfold into

wings. Spits clean
the sword and lets go,

why she fled, how she
becomes fountain,

lush fruit, greening sea
between branches,

kelp forest, warm stone,
dark wood, the deep

quickening before spring.

Every Bird in My Blood Has a Name
— *in memory of m. e. e.*

Refuse
After all, I don't know what to give up or throw away.
In dreams, cats turn to dogs and my daughter, a stranger,
asks for change. My hands are veined plains. You are a
late sun, overgrazed, circled and sinking into the ground.

. . . electroshock therapy, which I have refused . . .

Relent
The light shudders with so
many moths, flinging at its gold.
What I don't let go will tangle
itself in the heart, spin rumors.
Set the husks of grief to tattle and burn.

Calibrate
Once there was just mountain breath. Now,
too many books trying to talk at once. Harbor
the bear in the brush quietly waiting.
I waited for you. Your tools and sleek script.
You could fix anything. How could I have failed?
In great tales, gods can be treacherous. Stop
trying to get it right. Descend.

Dearest friends,

*I have been sick for a long time. I have tried running
and art and medication, sleep and sex and breakfast
in a tent with the most glorious mountains waiting
for me outside. You lit my way here. You have gardened
me when I lost my roots, my soil.*

Culprit

The sky is

emptying

O, birds, where

... a bunch of dried weeds, decorated with beads and bells and slices of shells and nuts. It is simple and gentle, humorous and a little bit odd. It embodies the best of me ...

Antidote

Longed-for bewilderment. Our holy failures exposed.
Once you showed me a secret lake, so beautiful we
could have drowned in its shimmer, returned without
marrow, rebirthed outdoors, breathing through hollow
bones. We would sleep in sticks above the angry kin. We
would love

1. Worms 2. Cottonwood disguised as clouds 3. All things green

There is a deformity in me for which there is no remedy and with which I cannot live ... believe I am bad and will never be able to hear your protestations ...

I'm sorry for the grief I have caused ...

... here, my most precious possession ...

Psalm

In my dictionary of blood, ghosts. There is little
peace between branches of ice. I buried you
in winter under a cairn. So much night then.
To die and return is either grace or a lost
dream of warblers. This is the year of
disintegration. I gather maps in the shape
of a missing wing. A lift, a tilt. The flock's
ruthless return.

... called back home again ... there was nothing anyone could have done ...

Flo and the Frozen Girl

The "NIH-owned" chimps in the medical research unit in Alamogordo are awaiting sanctuary after US Fish and Wildlife made them endangered species in 2015.

Pauline rescues puppies born under a board in the barn.

She reads about the chimps used in medical research awaiting sanctuary.

She dreams she is a girl covered in snow. Standing frozen in the road.

Pauline reads that Flo is the oldest chimp in Alamogordo. She was captured in Africa and put in a zoo, then a circus, then used as a breeder for medical research.

Pauline pretends to smile in public. She feels weighed down in skin, encapsulated.

Over the years, Pauline reads, Flo gave birth to four babies. (The article says chimp babies typically nurse for four to five years and stay in the nest with their mother for seven to eight years.) Pauline hopes Flo planted a small forest in each of their hearts before they were taken away after birth.

Pauline tells her doctor she is tired all the time. Frozen girl says, *Ah, lo, baba.*

Young chimps, Leo and Horace (named by researchers in a different facility), felt pain, like thimbles of fire placed in their muscles and joints for "a muscle movement study."

Pauline dreams she gives birth to a bird. Her priest says, *We don't know what heaven looks like.*

    Goal directed is the term used in psychiatry to mean "probably not suicidal."

    Many of the captive chimps, Pauline reads, have died gruesome deaths.

When Pauline was born, her mother said prayers and handed her back to the nuns.

    Flo is over fifty years old when she becomes an endangered species.

Pauline takes the puppies out of the maw and makes a nest of her coat. She feeds them milk in eyedroppers.

    Flo paces her cage and does not sleep.
    Pauline reads how an orangutan tries to save a man in snake-infested waters.

Leo and Horace hang on the struts of their cages in the article's photo.
    Pauline makes a goal to watch less TV. Frozen girl has a face.
    There are no words for what might thaw in her.

Guest Place in the Shadow
— after Brigit Pegeen Kelly (1951–2016)

Fat with brag, airwaves bloat.
The demagogue has won
his argument. Meanwhile,
ghosts hammer at dream
docks where my father is
half beast. I walk my early
cities grateful for gray, loving
what I would too soon lose.
The past calls, cranes bugling
the lathered light. Cloud flocks
graze fallow fields, shrouds of
leaves gold the ground. My friend
who just died invites me in for a swim.

There I Stood, in All My Forms

Until I Could No Longer Fly and So Became a Map: Pegasus

Just before prayer, my mother slept
in a sea of snakes, her holy, her grist,

bone meal and blood. I swam between her
continents of heartbeat and lung. She was throat

pulled open and slit; her quieted voice
made me winged, and I fled from that nape,

I flew. Through clouds small as fists I rose,
serpents taut as tongues on my back.

Cinched by men who wanted the sun,
I rode them out of the stone of her gaze.

My mother's song a hover and flame, in barracks
on the ground. I wanted to gallop and nap,

wanted to feed at her feet. How she bled down
the stairs like pomegranates, her hands rising

in prayer, before the death of my birth: fetlock
and dock, withers and croup.

My shadow a streambed, my glass into stars. Old
now, I flank a map. I am muzzle of plains.

In these days of war, rivers glint
my haunches. I drink from oceans

of the missing and yearned. I am hobble
and bruise in the dark dirt. My mother, my maker,

now daybreak and flaw. Smoke and flower
flush-plucked out of her gaping hands.

From the Island of Pomegranates

Dear dead daughters,
The tide has brought a nymph—
hungry, poor child, timid
and sharp-clawed as a bird.
Her eyes a shade of sea.
We feed her the seeds carefully:
peeled fruit makes crimson
her mouth when the pale rind
is spent. She leaves us
a drowning sun, fins
we find in sand. Our days
steeped in stain, salt washed.
Around us fruits dangle
like the faces of girls.

Pandora on the Mother Road

I am the smiling saint of Central Avenue. Here gravel sings to trees and the sun grants me a law degree. I see the road they call mother sneak into her rivery dress at night, and goodness me does she flow black oil. Feathers of crows laugh darkness in the trees. I am cut stone without a heart to break. A woman who can feast on smells: biscuits and chicken grease, cinnamon rolls, fries: they pipe them out for free. My daughter used to bring me goodwill blankets, but now those snooty kids in "outreach team" orange arrive. I'm sure I can outreach any of them cuz I play this piano score all the way to California and back. Not that I've left this trash can in twenty years, but the ocean visits here in wild storms. My can of mirrors, if you dare to look, holds my mother's faces. I walk from Yale to Harvard to further my education. Loco brings me pints of strong stuff, and we laugh at tourists, hold out our hands. When I still and bird-perch myself on this branch of dirt, I am beautiful. Grit in my teeth and gods in my hair.

Atlas

and like, or unlike God, he was always
with us, among the lush, ongoing trees
— Susan Aizenberg

Not cake or crook, not graft or
gauze, not a twin engine or double-
edged sword, not the orange moon posing
as fruit on the horizon, or the table of sweets she

forbade, not night's eyes while he stood
still as glass, not the round weight in his hands held over
his head, not the steady watch of the man with a knife,
or the blue graze of his mother in her den.

The boy could only dream of apples, paring the skin
from its dense meat, the first sweet bite,
the seeded core. He held his arms high until
the fall, the knife, *loser* carved

onto his tablet of skin.
Later, his smiling face in newsprint. Such a nice
boy, his teachers will say. O little Atlas, our world
in your thin arms while we slept.

There I stood begging at the door of my death

She was vessel, light as spore, mad as a muskrat rooting for crumbs in the sheets, *querida tengo hambre*, she burrowed deep-blanketed in a room full of doors she didn't dare, through one a view of her swath of land in Silver City where her double wide sat mouthing curse words at the dry wind. *My mother helped build the bomb and I well I. Birthed hundreds of babies silk and wet as sea creatures only a few came out blue and I breathed weather into their tiny lungs, her exterminated souls, unburnt and decindered, mewling back out from the muck. My father was a stutter, a man of too many secrets that poked at his tongue and made it shudder.* Patient has dementia heart failure diabetes hypertension depression psychosis. Patient refuses medications on a regular basis. Patient is rude to the nurses when they try to feed her though seems to be hungry. *No me dan nada aqui, call my sister to get me out of here. The dumb ones are the meanest.* Patient is aggressive and behaviors will be discussed in team. Medication is recommended for her multiple attempts at escape. *Oh my angels, bring me some cake, the smell of the sea, a moment of breath in the breeze, a rosary made of grapes. I dreamt I opened the door to my death and there I stood, in all my forms: a sea captain, a toothless witch, a mountain lion, a cough. There I stood begging.*

I Fled the Dry Lips of Men

A howling at the door
and ash from St. Helen on the sill.
Histology books were black
with mold, photos of pink cells
darkening. I did not own that body.
I did not want the fish to stop
swimming, the night to burn
and keep blowing away. Blue dreams
of drowning, the mountains hollowed
out, rivers on fire. I would never
give birth, so said my mother, thinning
after so many births and boys. Her sweet
poison a portent of shelter. When I
was a tree, she cut her initials in my trunk.
The life in me grew its own sky. I fled
the dry lips of men, the whiskered bite.
Harriers dropped feathers in my shade. Bark
gave way to hawk perch, to the certainty
I would survive only if empty. My daughter
would fly to me like a bird. Once steady
in the traffic of clouds and ash, she would land
in the silent crater of my hands.

Dermoid

Each night the silence.

Am I a mare?
        Am I ditch, late summer,
        dried mud?
    Am I murderer, muck?

I skull dark dreams
    with bits of spark,
        hunt ponds
    snaked with poachers.

Thirty before I stopped
    drowning, before
I began to feed
    as if I were a herd.

Am I fertilized,
    feckless,
        a farm?

    Metal splints in my toes,
        knee titanium-hinged,
pastures of organs gone missing.

    Strangers' hands still
        sound my mouth.

When they opened me
    and took her out,
    she was wound tight with hair
        and teeth, glandular.

        Fingered with
    bark from the trees
I tried to grow in there.

Dear Human,

My hands are wild
as willow and as raw.
School was a series of book
smells and subtitles. Never
quite right, a rock in the
shoe.

Last week I seized
and gave birth to
a lynx. Between
my breasts, a vase
with fresh soil.
Under my ribs
my brother lies
in peace. When
you say, *Hands
up!* I cradle him
in the suitcase
of my throat.

For my own good
night took all her food
out of the fridge and
smashed the glop on the walls,
the color of spleen. It was beautiful
before the police arrived. The rope
confessed the crime, razor blade,
sun, shoddy door in a motel
room. The web, the cage, the closet.

Shoot me here, in
my garden's body.
My wings blew off last
week in a storm.

The Flying Boy

My father, who sang only
at night, baptized me there
and sent me to sail. It's true
I sought the sun, that its heat
caused me to melt. But breathless,
my father's first touch, his prayer against
flesh, how he bowed and plucked,
how he toiled. What could I do?
He took tallow and pressed
my soft sinew of back into wings,
furrowed by feathers plucked
from the hawk I brought
home from the hills.
I shook my shoulders wide and sailed high
so he could see I was more
than he knew, boundless,
a flying boy. Not the soft down of
my arms, but something hollow
lifted me up.
I wanted to vanish in smoke.
Only this moment of call-
and-response, his fingered
faith, my rise, and the heat of
my fall past farmers tilling
the ground, my watery breath,
my feathers afloat on the sea.

Wearing His Father's Dog Tags

The boy keeps sailing over the flooded fields
frothing with ditch: steam rising, hot ground under
the wet. Cottonwoods the width of a hut twist
into themselves, a century of bark.

He slips fingers into islands of slime, bays
where cool bugs hunker. He is small boy boat,
destination third grade, arms beginning
to muscle. He hopes to see a great white shark

someday. He unclasps crawdads from the muck.
Smell of dead greens against the stile. The field
now pond with grain tips swimming. Air frilled
with buzz and bite. Here in drought, water abounds.

Birthed from the first waters, his head was
soaped with sludge from the womb. The room:
full of ghosts. This boy gleams with tree sap,
sand glass, places sea sedge and carp

on the deck. He is hoisting the sail, departing
his shore. His father has long stopped waving.
His mother: steady as tree, beacon and branch.
The boy keeps sailing, a horizon they can't see.

Feathers Appear on Branches as Flame

Stone
Once a river, bedded in silt.
Once a bed, a bank, a rolling thing.
Palm of afterbirth, of stile.

⊟⊟

It is the year of bees and of men
stepping on the moon.
A branch cracks, and the night slivers
into shards of blue and gold.

Ditch
Revive
trash and tumble,
the tongue
of water
always sung.

⊟⊟

The fractured wood smells sweet,
like new skin. Its limbs are wet, and the
horses will not go near it again.

Tree
Coat of birds.
Let the owl stare
encircled in burn.

⊟⊟

Days later, the tree swarms
with hive. How thin
the skin of girls. How we
will open our mouths
for the sting.

Dirt

It all ends here.
Comets, oceans.
The liquid stroke
of living. You must
learn to live with less.

☷☷

And When He Thought He Had Found Me

I sought the ocean floor
sequins of light on the surface
my veined wings enough trouble
for one nymph who is not ghost
death or dirt or starting
to melt   always young   bound
to the unexpected afterlife of whales
I was held hostage in a photograph
once   buried myself in stars
dying in the muck in the steady
drip drip
not ghost but clouds where I drown
my gods and their feats

In the Tree Museum

Linoleum the color of snow,
our lit feet bleached
in fluorescence. We hold
still in no breeze, the clean
trees do not smell of pine. A speaker
chants the names of the missing:

"Rosewood, Crepe Myrtle, Mahogany,
Yellow Wood, Oil Palm, Ponderosa,
Apple, Pear, Star-Anise,
Muttonwood, Lychee, Locust"

(The lookalike pines speak.)

We are snag tongue trunk
burn   rock pile wash
A wing a spout
a space
between beak and bark
A hen a hive a nest a trough
A storm a stool a limb
page frame ghost
fire logjam violin

(An old woman tells her story.)

*My mother was a cottonwood tree. Her rough bark, her mast and
spires. At night I slept in the sad planks of my father's home, drowning
in brown stain, its crackings. By day I sailed the seas in my tree, my
true, my shade, my ditch-bound. I learned root, breeze, season.*

"Lime, Snot Apple, Peppermint,
Purple heart, Tulip Tree, Walnut,
Water gum, Willow, Yew, Yucca,
Cannonball, Cashew, Bristlecone"

birds nested   hatched   fledged in her green
arms   I watched her leaf   become bone again
My mother was a cottonwood tree
in her the spell
of spring, the rise
of spiders
the buzz, the hum
the sprig
the warm
snow of her cotton

"Oleander, Orchid, Spruce,
Olive, Paloverde, Tea Tree,
Peach, Paperbark, Oak,
Sequoia, Hemlock, Pomegranate"

We are bottlenecked   dirt
starved   clear cut

The voices stop, we shuffle.
Underground, a rumbling.

The Painter

My neighbor on 4th and Bell,
after a drenched night's binge,
opened the blue mouth

of her fridge, threw plates
and mugs of food at the wall:
an abstract of mustard, milk,

macaroni and cheese. Greens dripping
from soup and meat in its grease.
She wanted to go to Barcelona.

Or Buenos Aires. Some faraway
city where the sea was full of fish.
She sat on her hands

to evade the bind. The
men were gentle, clipped
each thin wrist into silver-

ringed cuffs, then she bent
her head down for the flashing
car outside.

I think of her often when rage
ascends. When I want to break
everything I have. How the heart

pumps buried in body's thick heat,
and nothing at night can fill it:
nothing but longing, nothing but blood.

Martia
— *in memory of l. s.*

Under the sky of your family home, you found a tumor on your chest.
Cells coughed a net of stars until you, as a girl, wound red and white
yarn around the trees like veins. Your horse nuzzled the scar, staunch-
ing the hurt after it detonated like a bomb. Your mother went missing
with her milk. Later the mass was missing its mate. Before you died,
you told me of the hawk who dropped feathers on your head, some
sign, you thought, from the heavens that the gods were softening their
approach. You joined yourself to the girl with red, meaning stitches of
blood. You called out for your mother in a storm of dust, and in her
magnificent arms of night you were gone.

Avalanche
— *in memory of k. p.*

Think of me final   think of me
fast   of fracture   flame of crust
cold and folded over
the rise and fall
of generation   of tumble and low
the whirl   the wave   the slack
and the spin. I remember you
young   tasting earth with
your feet   the girth and heft of hills.
Have you loved enough the smell and
lick of storm   the hymns of dirt
and pine   the rise   the crest
the summits now sung in snow?
Bed the boom   the breath   the lavish
white of your vanishing

Machu Picchu

Once I was a cottonwood's captain.
Her split-trunk cocoon smooth as skin, barkless.

My mates were bald boys and wild, dirty girls.
We sailed across the bland fields to you,

verdant beacon, cut-glass spires of stone.
My steep steps, my granite prayers.

The ditches ran with fury. In night's splintered light,
my father simmered. He chased us into trees

where we set off again. O clouds above the squall.
Over our own piney mountains, dry with baked dirt.

We ate soup right out of the can. Made maps in mud.
Rose to the occasion of you when we were able.

a guide to tongue tie surgery

Notes

"A Guide to Tongue Tie Surgery" (4): Tongue-tie surgery involves cutting the short, tight piece of skin connecting the underside of the tongue to the bottom of the mouth. It's a quick, simple, and almost painless procedure that usually improves breastfeeding straight away for infants and speech and oral health in children and adults.

"Metronome and Daruma Doll" (27): A daruma doll is a hollow round Japanese traditional doll modeled after Bodhidharma, who founded the Zen tradition of Buddhism. The dolls are seen as symbols of perseverance and good luck.

"Saint Ursula" (35) has many legends; here is the one that inspired the poem:

> Ursula, the daughter of a Christian king in Britain, was
> asked in marriage by the son of a pagan king. She, desiring
> to remain unwed, got a delay of three years, which time she
> spent on shipboard, sailing about the seas; she had ten noble
> ladies-in-waiting, each of whom, and Ursula, had a thousand
> companions, and they were accommodated in eleven vessels.
> At the end of the period of grace, contrary winds drove
> them into the mouth of the Rhine, they sailed up to Cologne
> and then on to Bâle (Basle in Switzerland), where they
> disembarked and then went over the Alps to visit the tombs
> of the apostles at Rome. They returned by the same way to
> Cologne, where they were set upon and massacred for their
> Christianity by the heathen Huns, Ursula having refused to
> marry their chief. The barbarians were dispersed by angels,
> the citizens buried the martyrs and a church was built in
> their honor by Clematius. "The inherent logistic improba-
> bilities of moving such a company are obvious, especially
> given the chaos of the mid 5th century, to which the medieval
> legend assigns their martyrdom at the hands of the Huns."
> — Alban Butler et al., *Lives of the Saints*
> (New York: P. J. Kennedy and Sons, 1956)

"Little Robber Girl" (40) is a character in Hans Christian Anderson's story "The Snow Queen."

"Why did you kill your wife, mr XYZ?" (43) was inspired by the myth of Narcissus in Ovid's *Metamorphoses*. Ovid was an eighth-century AD writer whose Latin narrative poem *Metamorphoses* contains over 250 myths with themes such as transformation, violence, love, loss, and power.

"West Side Murders, Seven Years Later" (47) contains information from an *Albuquerque Journal* article published on February 1, 2016, and was inspired by Joseph Cornell's shadow box *Untitled (Bébé Marie)*.

"How She Becomes a Fountain" (50) is inspired by the stories of Arethusa and Triptolemus from Ovid's *Metamorphoses*.

"Until I Could No Longer Fly and So Became a Map: Pegasus" (59) was inspired by the myth of Medusa and Pegasus in Ovid's *Metamorphoses*.

"From the Island of Pomegranates" (60) and "And When He Thought He Had Found Me" (000) were inspired by the many mentions of nymphs in Ovid's *Metamorphoses*.

"Dermoid" (65): A dermoid is a sac-like growth in the body—in this case the ovary—that contains structures such as hair, fluid, teeth, and glands.

"The Flying Boy" (67) is inspired by the myth of Icarus in Ovid's *Metamorphoses*.

Acknowledgments

Grateful acknowledgment is made to the editors of the following publications where these poems, some of which have been subsequently revised, originally appeared:

ABQ inPrint: "Mud Babies" and "Monster"

Book of Matches: "Machu Picchu"

Bosque, the Magazine: "West Side Murders, Seven Years Later," "There I stood begging at the door of my death," and "Anatomy of Silence"

Creative Santa Fe, Moment Booklet: Transformation: "Avalanche"

Cutthroat, A Journal of the Arts: "Heaven" (second-place winner in the Joy Harjo Poetry Contest, 2020) and "From the Island of Pomegranates"

Dark Mountain Review: "Fin Feather Bark and Skin"

deLuge Literary and Arts Journal: "Cigarette Smoke and a Blue Impala"

Equinox: "Ghost Town on Iris Avenue"

Fence: "Sheltering in Place for Beginners" and "As the Numbers of Dead Rise, Moths Fill the Room"

Fixed and Free Anthology: "Pandora on the Mother Road" and "Flo and the Frozen Girl"

Hunger Mountain: "The Embassy of Silence"

Literary Mama: "At the Rest Stop, Fully Gloved, She Calls Me Mommy"

Mom Egg Review: "My Mother as Moon" and "Until I Could No Longer Fly and So Became a Map: Pegasus"

Telebooth Project: "Dear Human," and "Dermoid"

NM Audubon Society Facebook Post: "Martia"

The Nonbinary Review: "Snow Queen"

Psaltery and Lyre: "Saint Ursula"

SWWIM: "A Guide to Tongue Tie Surgery"

Voices in the Museum of Trees (book): "In the Tree Museum"

This book, in many ways, is a collaboration, as so many poets and others have contributed energy and critiques to these poems.

Much gratitude to the fabulous team at the University of New Mexico Press, especially Elise McHugh, James Ayers, Anna Pohlod, Isaac Morris, and Min Marcus.

Thank you to my stalwart poetry-group members, whose brilliant comments have lifted these poems up and given them buoyancy: Mary Morris, Barbara Rockman, Gary Worth Moody, Donald Levering, Robin Hunt, and Debbie Casillas in Santa Fe; and David Meischen, Cindy Huyser, Eileen Lawrence, and Scott McDonald in virtual, long-distance gatherings.

Thank you to my mentors, Amy Beeder, Lise Goett, Lynn Miller, and Hilda Raz, for your ever abiding faith in my work and your careful critiques, and to Mark Wunderlich and Jane Hirschfield for your assistance with some of the poems in this book.

Gracias a mi hermana poeta, Katherine DiBella Seluja, whose poems and companionship bring daily joy and inspiration as well as lots of laughter.

Endless love and hugs to Lynda Miller, Sandi Stromberg, Laurie Hause, Cindy Sylvester, Jill Root, and Stella Reed for your creative inspirations and ebullient support.

Thank you to Lene Kilde for your glorious sculpture, whose image graces the cover of this book.

Deep appreciation to Edie Tsong for writing with me every week and reminding me to make space on the page for the breath.

And to Tres, my love and life partner, I'm grateful every day for your support, editing help, and fierceness.

And gratitude to my ancestors who sing to me when I am lost, and to the trees who raised me.